From:

Inspire Books is an imprint of Peter Pauper Press, Inc.
Spire is a registered trademark of Peter Pauper Press, Inc.

All phtotographs copyright ©
Getty Images

For scriptural references, please see last pages.

Designed by Karine Syvertsen

Copyright © 2005
Peter Pauper Press, Inc.
202 Mamaroneck Avenue
White Plains, NY 10601
All rights reserved
ISBN 1-59359-964-1
Printed in China

7 6 5 4 3 2 1

Visit us at www.peterpauper.com

GOD
in all
Seasons

TWELVE MONTHS OF BLESSINGS

INTRODUCTION

God is with you and within you in every season and in every month—and indeed in every day of the year.

Let us therefore celebrate not only Easter, Christmas, and secular holidays, but also all those days in between, confident in the blessings of a wonderful God. And as we celebrate holidays (and all those special but ordinary days) with feasts and fun or with peaceful, quiet joy, let us always have the clear sense of God's presence touching our lives.

S. M. H.

There is a time for everything, a season for every activity under heaven.

ECCLESIASTES 3:1 NLT

WINTER

Time performs a solemn dance in winter. Daylight hours melt quickly into longer nights, so that the days before the holidays seem to fly by, but the latter half of winter drags by interminably, no matter what the groundhog says. Yet seed catalogs arrive by mail, along with summer cottage rental brochures. And January's thaw suggests something more is to come, too.

For in those longer winter nights lies a promise from God—a promise of a new year with new beginnings and opportunities. Thus winter becomes a time to plan, to reflect, to work anew. Birds are busy at the feeders. The oven warms the kitchen with constant baking. Cozy fires and comfy quilts hold heat and hearts together. What could be better than celebrating winter?

January

✿

The first month of every year ushers in a sense of newness—a new year, a new beginning to revitalize self and relationships, faith and fortitude. We often use the month of January to recommit ourselves to a weight loss or exercise program, to resolve to end old habits and begin new ones. Resolutions and January go hand in hand.

A new year. We have started it.
Only the Lord knows
if we will finish it. Let us live every
day as if it were our last
opportunity to serve our Saviour.
That way this year will be the best
year we have ever lived.

STANLEY BARNES

Be transformed
by the renewing of your
mind, that you may
prove what is that good
and acceptable and
perfect will of God.

ROMANS 12:2 NKJV

You must renew your determination regularly. . . . Clocks need winding, cleaning, and oiling. Sometimes they need repair. Similarly, we must care for our spiritual life by examining and servicing our hearts at least annually.

FRANCIS DE SALES

[God] can shatter old habits, blast apart old attitudes, wash away old resentments and hurts, push aside old fears and limitations and stereotypes. It's His energy, His power, that's at work in our lives.

CHARLES SWINDOLL

True newness never comes from us, from the natural. It comes from beyond us, from the God with whom we have the privilege of walking. Our response has to be: Everything is new under the Son, for it is He who makes all things new.

DENNIS F. KINLAW

We pray that with his power God will help you do the good things you want and perform the works that come from your faith.

2 THESSALONIANS 1:11 NCV

February

The ancient Romans observed a mid-February feast day with a lottery drawing that paired up Rome's single men and women. Centuries later the church tied this feast day to Saint Valentine, the patron saint of lovers. In this, the shortest month, let Saint Valentine's Day and your love for others remind you of God's love, too.

God's grace is
the oil that fills the
lamp of love.

HENRY WARD BEECHER

Love does not make you weak, because it is the source of all strength, but it makes you see the nothingness of the illusory strength on which you depended before you knew it.

BLOY

*Love is the active concern
for the life and growth
of that which we love.*

ERICH FROMM

*Respect is what we owe;
love, what we give.*

PHILIP JAMES BAILEY

I say to you,
love your enemies.
Pray for those who hurt you.
If you do this,
you will be true children
of your Father in heaven.

MATTHEW 5:44–45 NCV

Love is an act of will, both an intention and an action.

M. SCOTT PECK

Where there is love and wisdom, there is neither fear nor ignorance.

FRANCIS OF ASSISI

Let us stop just saying we love each other; let us really show it by our actions.

1 JOHN 3:18 NCV

March

In the fourth century a teenager named Patrick was kidnapped from his home in England and forced into slavery in Ireland. A daring escape six years later returned the young man to his home. But one night Patrick dreamt about a man who begged him to return to Ireland and preach the Gospel. After several years of Bible study, Patrick did just that, returning to Ireland as a missionary.

For the remainder of his life, Patrick traveled throughout Ireland, planting churches and baptizing thousands of new believers, despite violent opposition from the largely pagan civil authorities. As you celebrate Saint Patrick's Day, remember this selfless young man and follow his example. Wear the green, white, or orange of the Irish flag on this holiday and share God's love with others.

*You shall receive power
when the Holy Spirit has
come upon you; and you
shall be My witnesses both
in Jerusalem, and in all
Judea and Samaria,
and even to the remotest
part of the earth.*

ACTS 1:8 NASB

God's might to direct me,

God's power to protect me,

God's wisdom for learning,

God's eye for discerning,

God's ear for my hearing,

God's Word for my clearing.

SAINT PATRICK

O Ireland, isn't it grand you look—
Like a bride in her rich adornin'?
And with all the pent-up
love of my heart
I bid you the top o' the morning!

JOHN LOCKE

God never shuts one door but He opens another.

IRISH PROVERB

May the road rise to meet you,
May the wind be always at your back,
May the sun shine warm
upon your face,
And rains fall soft upon your fields,
And, until we meet again,
May God hold you
in the palm of His hand.

<small>Traditional Irish blessing</small>

SPRING

The touch of God's hand is evident in spring. Birds, squirrels, chipmunks, and bugs respond busily to the gradual advance of longer days and warmer weather. Green shoots poke their heads through gray leafy leftovers. The odor of fresh cut grass replaces the stale, smudgy smell of winter ash and salt.

It's time to air the blankets, to think about planting a garden, to take an impromptu picnic. For a long walk, a sweater is still needed to ward off the chill that lingers after winter's demise. But the touch of God's hand is evident in the crocus and the robin. Spring has come with newness of life. Let's celebrate!

April

April often plays host to the joyous Christian celebration of Easter, for hidden within April's green warmth is the promise of new life, new beginnings, new reasons to celebrate. Let April's promise of newness bring Easter to your soul.

Let us never forget that after every Friday of sorrow comes your promised Sunday of joy. Praise the Lord—for the Son is truly risen!

B. J. HOFF

Easter is not a passport to another world; it is a quality of perception for this one.

W. P. LEMON

The angel answered and said to the women, "Do not be afraid, for I know that you seek Jesus who was crucified. He is not here; for He is risen, as He said. Come, see the place where the Lord lay."

MATTHEW 28:5–6 NKJV

Christ lives in us today;
and because He lives
in us Easter is more than
a celebration: it is a
day of victory, a day of
renewed hope and joy
and promise.

ABRAM MILLER LONG

Now let the heav'ns be joyful,
Let earth her song begin,
Let the round world keep triumph
And all that is therein;
Invisible and visible,
Their notes let all things blend;
For Christ the Lord hath risen—
Our Joy that hath no end.

JOHN OF DAMASCUS

*During the forty days
after his crucifixion,
[Jesus] appeared to the
apostles from time to time
and proved to them in
many ways that he
was actually alive.*

ACTS 1:3 NLT

May

In 1915 Congress set aside the second Sunday of May as a national holiday celebrating mothers. Since that time Mother's Day has become the busiest day of the year for restaurants, the third-largest card-selling holiday in the nation, and one of the year's busiest long-distance telephone calling days. But, at heart, it is a time to say "Thank you, Mom," for all the love and nurturing she has bestowed on you. May and Mother's Day—what wonderful reasons to celebrate!

She knows the lowest prices, everybody's birthday, what you should be doing, and all your secret thoughts . . . And when you have tried her patience and worn her out, you can win her back with four little words, "Mom, I love you!"

WILLIAM A. GREENBAUM II

She watches over the
affairs of her household and does
not eat the bread of idleness.
Her children arise and call her
blessed; her husband also,
and he praises her.

PROVERBS 31:27–28 NIV

A mother is the truest friend we have. When trials, heavy and sudden, fall upon us; . . . still will she cling to us, and endeavor by her kind precepts and counsels to dissipate the clouds of darkness, and cause peace to return to our hearts.

WASHINGTON IRVING

*Honor your father
and mother, as the LORD
your God commanded you.
Then you will live a
long, full life in the land
the LORD your God
will give you.*

DEUTERONOMY 5:16 NLT

A Recipe for a Loving Mother

Take a large bowl of grace.
Sprinkle with kindness. Add a dash
of smiles and a heap of love.
Throw in a dash of forgiveness and
a splash of gentleness for flavor.
Stir together throughout the years.
Serves innumerable children.

STEPHANIE MICHELE

June

Though many states had already begun to honor fathers, it was not until 1966 that President Lyndon Johnson declared the third Sunday of June as a national Father's Day. Now cards, neckties, and barbecues help us remember the men who have influenced our lives. Enjoy June, and honor your father.

The words a father speaks to his children in the privacy of the home are not overheard at the time, but, as in whispering galleries, they will be clearly heard at the end and by posterity.

RICHTER

Fathers, do not exasperate your children; instead, bring them up in the training and instruction of the Lord.

EPHESIANS 6:4 NIV

What a heritage to pass on to our children . . . memories of home intertwined with memories of praise and laughter and song and the strong, undergirding arms of the living God.

JACK HAYFORD

The most important thing a father can do for his children is to love their mother.

THEODORE M. HESBURGH

*The righteous man walks
in his integrity; His children
are blessed after him.*

PROVERBS 20:7 NKJV

*Dads are the ones who bring
the healing hand of God when the
world breaks their kids' hearts.*

JOE WHITE

SUMMER

It's a wild time. Gardens are ripening; zucchini and tomato plants have invaded and produced more than expected. Lawns and weeds are growing way too fast. Flowerbeds are thick with blooms, and fireflies appear by the thousands, blinking their message to small children to "catch me if you can." It's a wild time. It's summer.

Yet it's a quiet time, too, filled with daydreams and plans, screened porches and rocking chairs, picnics and outdoor concerts, cookouts, and county fairs with cotton candy and caramel apples. Summer is hot and lazy, but the days go by too quickly. Come celebrate summer before its days are just a memory.

July

Half the year is over by the time the calendar reaches July, but America's favorite celebration is just beginning. Marching bands and parades, outdoor festivals and fireworks, picnics and impromptu baseball games are all a part of Independence Day. Our freedom is a sacred right, a gift to be treasured and celebrated.

We hold these truths to be self-evident, that all men are created equal, that they are endowed by their Creator with certain unalienable Rights, that among these are Life, Liberty, and the pursuit of Happiness. . . . And for the support of this Declaration, with a firm reliance on the Protection of Divine Providence, we mutually pledge to each other our Lives, our Fortunes and our sacred Honor.

THE DECLARATION OF INDEPENDENCE, JULY 4, 1776

*It was for freedom that Christ
set us free; therefore keep
standing firm and do not be
subject again to a yoke of slavery.*

GALATIANS 5:1 NASB

Proclaim liberty throughout all the land unto all the inhabitants thereof.

LEVITICUS 25:10 KJV
(THIS BIBLE VERSE WAS ENGRAVED
ON THE LIBERTY BELL IN 1753.)

Man is really free only in God, the source of his freedom.

SHERWOOD EDDY

I say to all men, what we have achieved in liberty, we will surpass in greater liberty. Steadfast in our faith in the Almighty, we will advance toward a world where man's freedom is secure.

HARRY S. TRUMAN

O beautiful for patriot dream
That sees beyond the years
Thine alabaster cities gleam
Undimmed by human tears!
America! America!
God shed His grace on thee
And crown thy good
with brotherhood
From sea to shining sea!

KATHARINE LEE BATES

August

August ushers in a period when Sirius, the Dog Star, rises at the same time as our sun. Because of this natural phenomenon, the ancients referred to the restful days of August as the "dog days" of summer. Whether you celebrate these "dog days" fishing, picnicking, or snoozing in a hammock, find plenty of rest and renewal in God, too!

All ordinances of Christian worship . . . are quiet resting-places. Far more than we are apt to realize do we need these silent times in our busy life, needing them all the more the busier the life may be.

J. R. MILLER

There remains therefore a rest for the people of God. For he who has entered his rest has himself also ceased from his works as God did from His.

HEBREWS 4:9–10 NKJV

Jesus knows we must come apart and rest awhile, or else we may just plain come apart.

VANCE HAVNER

Find rest, O my soul, in God alone; my hope comes from him.

PSALM 62:5 NIV

In a day when no matter who you talk to there is never enough time, cultivating an attitude of rest is the only way to survive the pressures with any semblance of serenity.

SARA WENGER SHANK

*Fishing is a chance to wash
one's soul with pure air . . .
It brings meekness and inspiration
from the glory and wonder of
nature . . . And it brings rejoicing
that one does not have to
decide a thing until next week.*

HERBERT HOOVER

September

Labor Day recognizes American workers and their contribution to the strength, prosperity, and well-being of our country. In 1894 Congress made the first Monday in September a national holiday to honor workers. Labor Day is also an unofficial reminder of summer's end, so whether you celebrate work or play this Labor Day, remember the blessings work brings.

He who labors as he prays lifts his heart to God with his hands.

St. Bernard of Clairvaux

*People go off to
their work; they labor
until the evening
shadows fall again.*

PSALM 104:23 NLT

*Good for the body
is the work of the body,
good for the soul is the
work of the soul, and
good for either the
work of the other.*

<small>HENRY DAVID THOREAU</small>

*Do not pray for tasks equal
to your powers; pray for powers
equal to your tasks!
Then the doing of your work
shall be no miracle,
but you shall be a miracle.*

Phillips Brooks

*Let the favor of the Lord
our God be upon us;
And do confirm for us the
work of our hands;
Yes, confirm the work
of our hands.*

PSALM 90:17 NASB

*The world is moved along,
not only by the mighty shoves
of its heroes, but also by the
aggregate of the tiny pushes
of each honest worker.*

ATTRIBUTED TO HELEN KELLER

AUTUMN

What an artist is our God! What a beautiful painting he makes of his creation in autumn. Chrysanthemums, dressed in their rusty oranges, snappy yellows, and light lavenders, bow in the breeze alongside crimson sumac and bold goldenrod. The reds, oranges, and yellows of the frost-tinged maples stand out as a bright splash against the deep forest green of pine and fir. The golden, hazy mist that clings to the distant hills mutes the colors of the trees to a periwinkle blue horizon. And even the grass wears the autumn color of a fresh-baked oatmeal cookie. In this season, God daubs the bright canvas of his world in rich colors. Celebrate God's artistry. Celebrate autumn's master-piece of color!

October

October brings to mind pumpkins and corn stalks, crisp autumn evenings, brilliant foliage, and golden harvest moons. As we ready ourselves for the cold winter months, let the warmth of the harvest celebration remind us of God's goodness and watchfulness over all.

*In the beginning you commanded
the earth, O Lord, to yield
green grass, herbs, and trees. . . .
If our barns are full, it is
because you have blessed us.
You have opened your hand.*

THOMAS BECON

*He who supplies seed
to the sower and bread for food,
will supply and multiply your seed
for sowing and increase the
harvest of your righteousness.*

2 CORINTHIANS 9:10 NASB

The red barn is filled with grain,
Cellar shelves hold treasures;
Oh, I am thankful to be living,
To share in autumn's pleasures.

EARLE J. GRANT

October is the fallen leaf,
but it is also a wider horizon more
clearly seen. It is the distant hills
once more in sight, and
the enduring constellations
above them once again.

HAL BORLAND

*Even now the reaper draws
his wages, even now he
harvests the crop for
eternal life, so that the
sower and the reaper
may be glad together.*

JOHN 4:36 NIV

Thine is the seed time: God alone
Beholds the end of what is sown;
Beyond our vision weak and dim
The harvest time is hid with him.

JOHN GREENLEAF WHITTIER

November

November brings a celebration that sets hearts singing. The generosity of our Creator, who has given us all that we need and enjoy, stirs our hearts to gratitude. As we thank others for their kindnesses throughout the year, let us on Thanksgiving Day also gratefully acknowledge God for everything he is, everything he does, and everything he provides.

We thank thee, then, O Father,
For all things bright and good,
The seed-time and the harvest,
Our life, our health, our food.
Accept the gifts we offer
For all thy love imparts,
And, what thou most desirest,
Our humble, thankful hearts.

MATTHIAS CLAUDIUS

*Oh, give thanks
to the LORD,
for He is good!
For His mercy
endures forever.*

Psalm 106:1 NKJV

Though right it is to give thanks,
True gratitude will live thanks!

ROBERT G. LEE

Always remember . . .
it is the spirit of giving that God
blesses—and a thankful heart.

MARGARET JENSEN

I will give thanks to the LORD because of his righteousness and will sing praise to the name of the LORD Most High.

PSALM 7:17 NIV

Thou who hast given so much to me, give one thing more—a grateful heart!

GEORGE HERBERT

December

December brings with it the bustle of readying home and hearth to celebrate Christmas. Yet the early days of December also herald another celebration—Advent. Advent calls us away from hurry, pointing us instead to a quiet, heartfelt, peaceful reflection of faith and spirit. To be truly ready to receive God's great gift of his Son, don't forget to celebrate Advent!

*The best way to begin
the Season of Advent is to take
an honest look within, and
see what changes might need to
be made . . . Amazing things can
happen . . . when one prepares
for the coming of royalty!*

STEVEN MOLIN

As he came to Bethlehem,
Even so Christ comes to them
Who with faithful hearts prepare
For the Lord to enter there.

ARDEN W. MEAD

*We who have so much to do seek quiet
spaces to hear your voice each day. . . .
We who are blessed in so many ways long
for the complete joy of your kingdom . . .
To you we say, "Come Lord Jesus!"*

HENRI J. M. NOUWEN

*The coming of the Christ Child is an invita-
tion to run to love, and so to learn to love.*

ANDREW M. WEYERMANN

For unto you is born this day in the city of David a Saviour, which is Christ the Lord. And this shall be a sign unto you; Ye shall find the babe wrapped in swaddling clothes, lying in a manger. And suddenly there was with the angel a multitude of the heavenly host praising God, and saying, Glory to God in the highest, and on earth peace, good will toward men.

LUKE 2:11–14 KJV

Angels, from the realms of glory,

Wing your flight o'er all the earth;

Ye who sang creation's story,

Now proclaim Messiah's birth:

Come and worship,

Come and worship,

Worship Christ, the newborn King!

James Montgomery

Scriptural References

Scripture quotations marked KJV are taken from the *King James Version* of the Bible.

Scripture quotations marked NASB are taken from the *New American Standard Bible*. Copyright © 1960, 1962, 1963, 1968, 1971, 1972, 1973, 1975, 1977 by The Lockman Foundation. Used by permission.

Scripture quotations marked NCV are taken from *The Holy Bible, New Century Version,* copyright © 1987, 1988, 1991 by Word Publishing, Dallas, Texas 75039. Used by permission.

Scripture quotations marked NIV are taken from the *Holy Bible, New International Version.* Copyright © 1973, 1978, 1984 by International Bible Society. Used by permission of Zondervan Publishing House. All rights reserved.